THE ULTIMATE METAL QUIZ
1st Edition
Copyright © 2023 of this edition
Manuel Latton

Cover design and conception:
Manuel Latton
Using an illustration from Freestock

Manuel Latton
Meylantstr. 15
44319 Dortmund
Germany
E-Mail: m.latton@yahoo.de

Manuel Latton

THE ULTIMATE METAL QUIZ

About The Book:

This quiz book THE ULTIMATE METAL QUIZ contains more than 200 questions from the noisy world of metal. Questions about classics, cult bands and famous personalities. It covers the entire history of metal. From the beginnings of metal to current releases. From super easy to really heavy. For beginners and experts. No questions about rock – just questions about metal!

The music quiz is designed for one, two or even more metalheads. Simply mark the appropriate answers next to the questions with a pencil and then add up the points at the end - who will be the new King Of Metal? With solution section at the end of the book.

Not only can you test your existing knowledge in a playful way, but you can also gain new metal classics and/or new background knowledge.

Attention is also paid to a wide coverage of the various subgenres such as heavy metal, power metal, thrash metal, death metal, black metal or nu metal.

If you would like to know more about the strongest albums and the best bands in metal, I recommend my book METAL - The 100 best albums of the 100 best bands or ROCK & METAL MADE IN GERMANY - The 50 best albums of the 50 best bands .

I hope you have fun puzzling, guessing, bragging and getting to know someone new.

Dortmund, November 2023

About The Author:

The author worked for years as an editorial staff member at a wide variety of rock and metal magazines, such as the online magazine stormbinger.at and/or the print magazine Legacy – The Voice From The Dark Side. He also contributed guest contributions to several other music magazines. He wrote many of his reviews or live reports under his then pseudonym Inhonorus.

Manuel Latton, born in 1988, lives in Dortmund with his wife and two daughters.

Published so far:

ROCK – The 100 best albums of the 100 best bands

METAL – The 100 best albums of the 100 best bands

ROCK & METAL MADE IN GERMANY – The 50 best albums of the 50 best bands

THE ULTIMATE ROCK QUIZ – Is your knowledge enough to pass this music quiz?

THE ULTIMATE METAL QUIZ

Manuel Latton

THE ULTIMATE METAL QUIZ

For my treasures Amy and Luna!

May these records help you find the right answers to all your questions, just as they helped me at the time.

1.

With which album did the German heavy metal legends Accept set a true milestone in 1982?

a. Under Jolly Roger

b. Keeper of the Seven Keys

c. Restless and wild

d. Battalions of Fear

2.

Which song wasn't written by the Swedish Melodic Death Metal flagship Amon Amarth?

a. Twilight of the Thunder God

b. From Afar

c. Death in fire

d. Ride For Vengeance

3.

With their debut album Tales From The Thousand Lakes, Amorphis present a fundamental album that influenced an entire genre! The album is still considered one of the best albums of...?

a. Death metal

b. Gothic metals

c. Doom Metals

d. Melodic Death Metal

4.

Which band cannot be classified as part of the New Wave Of British Heavy Metal (NWOBHM)?

a. Manilla Road

b. Angel witch

c. Saxon

d. Demon

5.

Sort these four Anthrax albums by release. The oldest album first. The youngest album last!

a. Among the living

b. Spreading the disease

c. For all kings

d. Stomp 442

6.

Angela Gossow was the brutal voice of Arch Enemy for a long time. Her vocals are still among the hardest female voices in music history, but in which city was she born?

a. London

b. Stockholm

c. New York

d. Cologne

7.

The Dutch Death-Doomers from Asphyx produced a wonderful neckbreaker with _____. Complete this sentence!

a. Last one on Mars

b. Last one on Saturn

c. Last one on Moon

d. Last one on Earth

8.

Chris Reifert is the mastermind of the cult death metal band from Autopsy. Which iconic band did he play drums for before forming Autopsy?

a. Death

b. Obituary

c. Deicide

d. Morbid angel

9.

What new subgenre of metal did Bathory's self-titled debut album usher in?

a. Thrash Metal

b. Death Metal

c. Black Metal

d. Heavy Metal

10.

Which famous artist did the cover of Benediction's Trancend The Rubicon?

a. Dan Seagrave

b. Derek Riggs

c. Ed Repka

d. Lemmy Kilmister

11.

Sort these four Black Sabbath albums by release. Oldest album first. The most recent album last!

a. 13

b. Black Sabbath

c. Paranoid

d. Master of Reality

12.

What is the name of the singer and co-founder of the band Blind Guardian?

a. Udo Dirkschneider

b. Hansi Kürsch

c. Kai Hansen

d. Tobias Sammet

13.

The death metal supergroup Bloodbath had some big names as singers, but who was the Swedes' very first singer?

a. Peter Tägtgren

b. Nick Holmes

c. Mikael Akerfeldt

d. Chris Reifert

14.

Which country does the death metal cult band Bolt Thrower come from?

a. Great Britain

b. USA

c. Sweden

d. Ireland

15.

Which album is not by Burzum?

a. Det som engang var

b. Hvis lyset tar oss

c. Aske

d. Sol

16.

Which dying beautiful doom metal song is on Candlemass's debut album Epicus Doomicus Metallicus?

a. Bewitched

b. At The Gallows End

c. A Cry From The Crypt

d. Solitude

17.

In which well-known Hollywood film did the Cannibal Corpse make a guest appearance in 1993?

a. Demolition Man

b. Ace Ventura

c. Rambo

d. Scream

18.

Which band did Celtic Frost come from?

a. Venom

b. Possessed

c. Hellhammer

d. Sodom

19.

What little special feature surrounds the debut album by the Norwegian black metallers Darkthrone?

a. The cover has no band name or title

b. On Soulside Journey the members already wore corpse paint

c. The debut album is classic thrash metal

d. The debut album is classic death metal

20.

Death's first long grooves were still pure death metal, but with which album did the sound develop more into technical death metal?

a. Human

b. Leprosy

c. Symbolic

d. Spiritual Healing

21.

What is special about Death Angel's thrash metal debut album The Ultra-Violence?

- a. The album came out pretty early (1980)

- b. Some of the musicians on the album are still 15 years old

- c. Half of the songs were written by Kirk Hammet

- d. The record is considered Australia's first thrash metal record

22.

White Pony is an album by the alternative/nu metal band....?

a. Korn

b. System Of A Down

c. Limp Bizkit

d. Deftones

23.

When was the debut album Deicide by the death metal band of the same name released?

a. 1990

b. 1991

c. 1989

d. 1988

24.

Why is the English band Demon considered a cult band in the underground, especially because of their debut album Night Of The Demon?

a. Because they have presented an underrated milestone in the field of death metal

b. Because they have presented an underrated milestone in the field of thrash metal

c. Because they have presented an underrated milestone in the New Wave of British Heavy Metal

d. Because they have presented an underrated milestone in the field of black metal

25.

Which big German thrash metal band released the first German thrash record with the EP Sentence Of Death?

a. Tankard

b. Destruction

c. Sodom

d. Kreator

26.

Dio is one of the most important rock and metal singers in music history, but which band was he never in?

a. Rainbow

b. Dio

c. Heaven & Hell

d. Deep purple

27.

Which of the following albums is not one of the founding records of Swedish death metal?

a. Left Hand Path

b. The Nocturnal Silence

c. Like An Everflowing Stream

d. Into the Grave

28.

Another cult band of black metal is Jon Nödtveidt's Dissection. Which song did Mr. Nödtveidt contribute guest vocals to?

a. Necrophobic – Nailing The Holy One

b. Grave – You'll Never See

c. Kreator – Extreme aggression

d. Entombed - Drowned

29.

Disturbed presented a more than successful cover version of the song Sound Of Silence in 2015. Who did the song originally come from?

a. Bob Dylan

b. Donovan

c. Simon & Garfunkel

d. Nick Drake

30.

Down are a supergroup in the field of sludge and southern metal, but what other bands did the supergroup consist of on their highly acclaimed debut album Nola?

a. Pantera, Corrosion Of Conformity, Crowbar, Eyehategod

b. Pantera, Alice In Chains, Crowbar, Kyuss

c. Pantera, Crowbar, Kyuss, Eyehategod

d. Pantera, Machine Head, Sepultura, Ministry

31.

Which subgenre can dream theater best be assigned to?

a. Doom metal

b. Gothic metal

c. Funeral Doom

d. Progressive metal

32.

In The Nightside Eclipse is another black metal masterpiece from 1994. But which Emperor member served a prison sentence for murder?

a. Ihsahn

b. Samoth

c. Tchort

d. Faust

33.

What did Entombed call themselves from 2014 after a dispute over the band's naming rights?

a. Entombed II

b. Entombed A.D.

c. Entombed Again

d. Entombed Entombed

34.

Which Metallica band member was also a founding member of Exodus' Bay Thrashers?

a. Lars Ullrich

b. James Hetfield

c. Kirk Hammett

d. Cliff Burton

35.

Besides Entombed, Dismember and Unleashed, which band is one of the Big Four of Swedish death metal?

a. Grave

b. Niefelheim

c. Necrophobic

d. Bloodbath

36.

What is the name of Gorgoroth's debut album?

a. Pentagram

b. Antichrist

c. Under The Sign Of Hell

d. Incipit Satan

37.

Sort these four Hammerfall albums by release. Oldest album first. The most recent album last!

a. Threshold

b. Renegade

c. Built To Last

d. Glory To The Brave

38.

Hatebreed is one of the most successful metal bands of the 2000s, but what is the name of the frontman of the American hardcore metallers?

a. Jonathan Davies

b. Corey Taylor

c. Jamey Jasta

d. David Drainman

39.

On which Helloween long record can you find the band's cult song I Want Out?

a. Keeper Of The Seven Keys – Part 1

b. Keeper Of The Seven Keys – Part 2

c. Walls Of Jericho

d. Master Of The Rings

40.

One of the most famous songs by the German pagan black metallers Helrunar is called _____? Complete this sentence.

   a. Älter als der Baum

   b. Älter als das Kreuz

   c. Älter als die Bible

   d. Älter als der Dom

41.

Join Me (In Death), Right Here In My Arms and Razorblade Kiss are songs by...?

a. HIM

b. Dio

c. Kiss

d. J.B.O

42.

What is the name of In Flames' debut album?

a. Colony

b. The Jester Race

c. Whoracle

d. Lunar Strain

43.

Which Iron Maiden record was the first with Bruce Dickinson behind the mic?

a. Killers

b. The Number Of The Beast

c. Piece Of Mind

d. Power slave

44.

Judas Priest is a true pioneering band of heavy metal. They are considered the first band from 1974…?

a. played heavy metal

b. released an album without a name or lyrics

c. developed the twin guitar sound with a second guitarist

d. played in complete darkness during performances

45.

Viva Emptiness, The Great Cold Distance and Discouraged Ones are albums by _____? Complete this sentence.

a. Katatonia

b. Paradise Lost

c. Opeth

d. November's Doom

46.

On which Korn album can you find the songs Falling Away From Me, 4U and Make Me Bad?

a. Korn

b. Life is a Peachy

c. Follow the leader

d. Issues

47.

With which album did the German thrash metallers Kreator reach first place in the German album charts for the first time?

a. Pleasure to kill

b. Gods Of Violence

c. Coma Of Souls

d. Phantom Antichrist

48.

Which of the following albums is not by Lake Of Tears?

a. Headstones

b. Forever Autumn

c. Veronica Decides To Die

d. A Crimson Cosmos

49.

With almost 30 million records sold (as of 2023), which album is the most successful debut album by a band in the current 21st century?

a. Korn – Korn

b. Slipknot - Slipknot

c. Disturbed – The Sickness

d. Linkin Park – Hybrid Theory

50.

Which thrash metal band did Robb Flynn release two albums with before starting Machine Head?

a. Violence

b. Forbidden

c. Whiplash

d. Nuclear Assault

51.

Crystal Logic is the name of an album by _____? Complete this sentence.

a. Manilla Road

b. Demon

c. Satan

d. Angel Witch

52.

Which band is the loudest band in the Guinness Book with a measured 139 decibels during a performance?

a. Manowar

b. Metallica

c. Deep purple

d. The Who

53.

Which statement about the Norwegian black metallers Mayhem is wrong?

a. They were involved in the church arsons in Norway in the early 1990s

b. Founding member Euronymous was murdered by Burzum mastermind Vikernes

c. Their first album was called Grand Declaration Of War

d. After Dead shot himself with a shotgun, Euronymous photographed his body to release it as the cover for the bootleg The Dawn Of The Black Hearts

54.

Which band was Megadeth mastermind Dave Mustaine briefly a member of?

a. Slayer

b. Exodus

c. testament

d. Metallica

55.

Another heavy metal classic is Dont Break The Oath by Mercyful Fate. Singer King Diamond was one of the first musicians....?

a. who practiced the stage dive

b. who wore corpse paint

c. who also took over the vocals as a drummer

d. who recorded his record entirely alone

56.

Which subgenres have had a significant impact on Metal Church?

a. Stoner and Southern Metal

b. Black and Death Metal

c. Speed and Thrash Metal

d. Groove and alternative metal

57.

Sort these four Metallica by release. Oldest album first. The most recent album last.

a. St Anger

b. Kill Em All

c. Metallica

d. Master Of Puppets

58.

Which country do the gothic metallers Moonspell come from?

a. Portugal

b. Spain

c. Greece

d. Italy

59.

Who was never a band member of Morbid Angel?

a. Terry Butler

b. Trey Azagthoth

c. Tim Yeung

d. Steve Tucker

60.

Which English rock band was Motörhead mastermind Lemmy Kilmister in before he founded Motörhead?

a. Slade

b. Cream

c. Hawkwind

d. The Rolling Stones

61.

Who isn't one of the Big Three of Doom Metal?

a. My Dying Bride

b. Paradise Lost

c. anathema

d. Saturnus

62.

Napalm Death even made it into the Guinness Book of Records – why?

a. Loudest band in the world

b. Most brutal covers in metal

c. Shortest song in the world

d. Longest song in the world

63.

On which Necrophobic long record can you find Before The Dawn, Unholy Prophecies and Inborn Evil?

a. Darkside

b. The Nocturnal Silence

c. Death to All

d. The Third Antichrist

64.

Who recorded the guitar tracks for the Swedish black metallers Nifelheim in the mid-1990s?

a. Jon Noedtveidt

b. Trey Azagthoth

c. Eric Hofmann

d. Jack Owen

65.

When were Nightwish founded?

a. 1994

b. 1995

c. 1996

d. 1997

66.

Slowly We Rot is the debut album by _____? Complete this sentence.

a. Morbid Angel

b. Obituary

c. Cannibal Corpse

d. Deicide

67.

Which Opeth album is considered a major musical turning point in the band's discography because it also incorporated jazz elements?

a. Heritage

b. Blackwater Park

c. Ghost Reveries

d. Deliverance

68.

Which band is not one of the Big Four of Thrash Metal?

a. Metallica

b. Megadeth

c. Overkill

d. Slayer

69.

After Ozzy Osbourne and Black Sabbath went their separate ways in the late 1970s and early 1980s, the Prince Of Darkness started a successful solo career. Which of the following songs from the debut album Blizzard Of Ozz was also released as a single?

a. I don't know

b. Goodbye to romance

c. Suicide solution

d. Mr. Crowley

70.

Pantera are one of the most successful groove metal / neo-thrash metal bands of the 1990s and are known for their hard songs. But what sound did they play on their first three to four albums in the early 1980s?

a. Thrash metal

b. Death metal

c. Speed and Power Metal

d. Heavy and glam metal

71.

At the beginning of the 1990s, Paradise Lost presented a true milestone in hard sound with Gothic. But which of the following band members is the singer?

a. Greg Mackintosh

b. Aaron Aedy

c. Nick Holmes

d. Stephen Edmondson

72.

Why is Paradise Lost's album Gothic such a special milestone?

- a. it was the first album to be released entirely in black

- b. It was the first album on which growls could be heard

- c. it is the first doom metal album in music history

- d. it is the namesake and founder of the Gothic Metal subgenre

73.

Seven Churches by Possessed is considered the birth of _____ in music history? Complete this sentence.

a. Thrash metal

b. Death metal

c. Black Metal

d. Heavy metal

74.

Sort these four Rammstein albums by their release. Oldest album first. The most recent album last.

a. Rosenrot

b. Liebe ist für alle da

c. Reise, Reise

d. Mutter

75.

Sabaton are one of the most successful power metal bands of the 2010s. Mainly their song lyrics are about _____. Complete this sentence.

a. the first and second world wars

b. about the Thirty Years' War

c. about the third world war

d. about the fight between humans and animals

76.

Saint Vitus are one of the first _____ in music history! Complete this sentence.

a. Thrash metal bands

b. Doom metal bands

c. Heavy metal bands

d. Black metal bands

77.

Sarcofargo are a cult metal band from Brazil. Which band did Sarcofargo mastermind Wagner Antichrist play in before he founded the band?

a. Anthrax

b. Sepultura

c. Overkill

d. Soulfly

78.

What is the correct name of Satan's debut album?

a. Court In The Act

b. Court In The Fact

c. Court In The Ract

d. Court In The Wact

79.

In 2006, the Danish doom metallers Saturnus released their fourth album, Veronica Decides To Die. Where does the album title come from?`

a. The album title is also the title of a book by Herman Hesse

b. The album title is also the title of a work by Paolo Coelho

c. The album title is also the title of a work by Richard Paul Evans

d. The album title is also the title of a work by Ernest Hemmingway

80.

When you hear the band name Savatage, the first thing that comes to mind is….?

a. The Number Of The Beast

b. Crazy Train

c. Hall Of The Mountain King

d. Easy Rider

81.

On which Saxon record can you find the song And The Band Played On?

a. Denim And Leather

b. Strong Arm Of The Law

c. Wheels Of Steel

d. Saxon

82.

Sepultura found their band name while translating a Motörhead song lyric. What was the name of the song?

a. Orgasmatron

b. Overkill

c. bomber

d. Dancing On Your Grave

83.

Six Feet Under every now and then releases a new part of their Graveyard Classics. What sets the series apart?

a. all death metal songs are instrumental

b. These are death metal songs that were actually written for horror films

c. Chris Barnes covers old rock hits like Jimi Hendrix in death metal style

d. They're all death metal ballads with clear vocals

84.

One of Skid Row's most famous songs is called...?

a. (Join Me) Into Death

b. Youth Gone Wild

c. Sweet Child O Mine

d. Animal (Fuck Like a Beast)

85.

Sort these four Slayer albums by release. Oldest album first. The most recent album last.

a. Hell Awaits

b. God Hates Us All

c. Season In The Abyss

d. Repentless

86.

What American state is a Slipknot album named after?

a. Georgia

b. Virginia

c. Iowa

d. Connecticut

87.

Which Ruhr metropolis do the German cult thrashers of Sodom come from?

a. Dortmund

b. Bochum

c. Gelsenkirchen

d. Essen

88.

With which wonderfully beautiful song did the Icelanders from Solstafir achieve their breakthrough?

a. Fjara

b. Lagnaetti

c. Otta

d. Dreamfari

89.

Who has never been a guest musician on a Soulfly song?

a. Fred Dust

b. Sean Lennon

c. Tom Araja

d. James Hetfield

90.

Suffocation were among the first bands to play _____! Complete this sentence.

a. Death metal

b. Brutal death metal

c. Technical Death Metal

d. Gore Death Metal

91.

Toxicity, Mezmerize and Hypnotize are albums by...?

a. Disturbed

b. Korn

c. System Of A Down

d. Slipknot

92.

Which of the following German thrash metal bands is still considered one of the Big Four of Teutonic Thrash?

a. Accuser

b. Holy Moses

c. Tankard

d. Angel Dust

93.

The Legacy is the thrash metal band's debut album...?

a. Exodus

b. Overkill

c. testament

d. Anthrax

94.

Troops Of Tomorrow, Beat the Bastards and Fuck The System are albums by...?

a. The Exploited

b. The Offspring

c. Black Flag

d. Suicidal Tendencies

95.

Which band, alongside Saint Vitus and Pentagram, is one of the co-founders of classic doom metal?

a. Reverend Bizarre

b. Trouble

c. Pagan altar

d. Abysmal Grief

96.

Which Type O Negative record achieved platinum status in 2000?

a. Slow, deep and hard

b. Dead again

c. October Rust

d. Bloody Kisses

97.

Why is Venom said to have such a big influence on the black metal scene?

a. Because they play black metal

b. Because they released one of the first black metal albums

c. Because they named an entire subgenre with the album and song name Black Metal

d. Because the singer always appeared in corpse paint

98.

What does the abbreviation and band name W.A.S.P. stand for?

a. White Anglo-Saxon Protestant

b. We Are Sexual Perverts

c. We Aint Sure, Pal

d. To this day we still don't know

99.

Which black metal band released the self-released demo Go Fuck Your Jewish God in 1998?

a. Gorgoroth

b. Watain

c. Dimmu Borgir

d. 1349

100.

Rob Zombie became famous in the early 1990s with the band _____! Complete this sentence.

a. White Zombie

b. Green Zombie

c. Red Zombie

d. Black Zombie

101.

In 1990, Into Darkness, Funeral Doom's first full-length, was released. What was the name of the band?

a. Summer

b. Spring

c. Winter

d. Autumn

102.

Which only Accept album won a gold record in the USA and Canada?

a. Restless And Wild

b. Balls To The Wall

c. Metal Heart

d. Blood Of The Nations

103.

Which of the founding members listed below is also the singer of Amon Amarth?

a. Ted Lundstom

b. Anders Hansson

c. Olavi Mikkonen

d. Johan Hegg

104.

Eclipse, Skyforger and Tales From The Thousand Lakes are albums by...?

a. Amorphous

b. Wintersun

c. Ensiferum

d. Moonsorrow

105.

Which statement is true! Compared to the other three bands in the Big Four of Thrash Metal (Metallica, Megadeth and Slayer), Anthrax…?

a. the band that was founded the latest

b. only had two founding members

c. not from San Francisco but from New York

d. not Americans but British

106.

On which Arch Enemy album did Alissa White-Gluz replace previous singer Angela Gossow?

a. Khaos Legions

b. War Eternal

c. Will to Power

d. Deceivers

107.

Asphyx's sound is a skillful mixture of...?

a. Death – and Black Metal

b. Thrash and Black Metal

c. Death and doom metal

d. Thrash and progressive metal

108.

Which of the following death metal records is not a cult record?

a. The Ten Commandments

b. Scream bloody gore

c. Altars Of Madness

d. Dying Of Everything

109.

Bathory is one of the biggest bands in black metal. But who was behind Bathory?

a. Cronos

b. Quorthon

c. Euronymous

d. Abbath

110.

Who used to be the singer of the English death metal band Benediction?

a. Barney Greenway from Napalm Death

b. Karl Willets from Bolt Thrower

c. Nick Holmes from Paradise Lost

d. David Vincent from Morbid Angel

111.

Which Black Sabbath albums were both the last of the Ozzy era and the first of the Dio era?

a. Paranoid - Forbidden

b. Headless Cross - Mob Rules

c. Never Say Die! –Heaven and Hell

d. Sabbath Bloody Sabbath – Tyr

112.

The Bard's Song, Mirror Mirror and And Then There Was Silence are cult songs by the German band...?

a. Blind Guardian

b. Scorpions

c. Grave Digger

d. Running wild

113.

What is the name of one of the biggest metal festivals in the world?

a. Wacken Open Air

b. Rock Am Ring

c. Rock In The Park

d. Rock in the hole

114.

After Bolt Thrower ended, Karl Willets joined _____ as a singer. Complete this sentence!

a. Kataklysm

b. Dark Tranquility

c. Vader

d. Memoriam

115.

Which band cannot be classified as True Norwegian Black Metal?

a. Darkthrone

b. Mayhem

c. Immortal

d. Cradle Of Filth

116.

Which Candlemass singer can be heard on the debut album Epicus Doomicus Metallicus?

a. Messiah Marcolin

b. Johan Langquist

c. Robert Lowe

d. Thomas Vikstrom

117.

Why have many of the Cannibal Corpse albums been indexed in Germany?

a. Because the music is just terrible

b. Because the music was way too loud

c. Because of the brutal cover artwork

d. Because of the brutal vocals

118.

Sort these four Celtic Frost albums and EPs by release. The oldest work first. The most recent work last.

a. Morbid Tales

b. To Mega Therion

c. Monotheist

d. Into The Pandemonium

119.

Which Darkthrone album is not part of Darkthrone's Unholy Trinity?

a. A Blaze In The Northern Sky

b. Under A Funeral Moon

c. Transylvanian hunger

d. Total death

120.

What was the name of the creative mind behind the cult death metal band Death?

a. Dimebag Darrell

b. Nicko McBrain

c. Chuck Schuldiner

d. Cliff Burton

121.

Which of these bands is not a neo-thrash metal band that was founded in the 2000s?

a. Warbringer

b. Heathen

c. Havok

d. Suicidal Angels

122.

Which of these Nu Metal albums saw the light of day first?

a. Slipknot - Slipknot

b. System Of A Down – Toxicity

c. Korn - Korn

d. Disturbed – The Sickness

123.

Which band has Deicide mastermind Glen Benton never been a guest singer with?

a. Slayer

b. Cannibal Corpse

c. Napalm Death

d. Cancer

124.

When was the high phase of the NWoBHM?

a. in the 1960s

b. in the 1970s

c. in the 1980s

d. in the 1990s

125.

Which album doesn't come from the German thrash metal legends Destruction?

a. Release From Agony

b. Eternal Devastation

c. Infernal overkill

d. Agent Orange

126.

The band Dio's debut album is called...?

a. Holy Driver

b. Holy Diver

c. Holy Diva

d. Holy Deliver

127.

Which death metal band cannot be classified as Swedish death metal?

a. Entombed

b. Dismember

c. Grave

d. Benediction

128.

Which song is from Dissection?

a. Where Dead Angels Lie

b. Freezing Moon

c. The Nocturnal Silence

d. Katharian Life Code

129.

Which Disturbed album was the most successful in Germany?

a. The Sickness

b. Believe

c. Asylum

d. Immortalized

130.

Which of the following bands cannot be classified as sludge metal?

a. Crowbar

b. Lynyrd Skynyrd

c. Eyehategod

d. Down

131.

Images And Words, Awake and Falling Into Infinity are albums by...?

a. King Crimson

b. Fate's Warning

c. Dream Theater

d. Rush

132.

Which black metal masterpiece appeared first?

a. Emperor - In The Nightside Eclipse

b. Gorgoroth – And The Sign Of Hell

c. Watain – Lawless Darkness

d. Mayhem – De Mysteriis Dom Sathanas

133.

Lars-Göran Petrov was the singer of the death metal band...?

a. Obituary

b. Entombed

c. Dismember

d. Vader

134.

What is the name of the debut album of the thrash metal band Exodus?

a. Fabulous disaster

b. Bonded By Blood

c. Blood in, blood out

d. Tempo Of The Damned

135.

Morgoth released a death metal classic with Cursed in 1991. Which country do Morgoth come from?

a. America

b. Sweden

c. Great Britain

d. Germany

136.

What was the name of the first singer of the black metal band Gorgoroth?

a. pest

b. Gaahl

c. Hat

d. Atterigner

137.

Which country do Hammerfall come from?

a. Sweden

b. Finland

c. Norway

d. Denmark

138.

Which album is from Hatebreed?

a. I Am Nemesis

b. Perseverance

c. All Hope Is Gone

d. Built To Last

139.

In which German city was Helloween founded in 1984?

a. Berlin

b. Hanover

c. Hamburg

d. Cologne

140.

Which band cannot be classified as Pagan Metal?

a. Varg

b. Moonsorrow

c. Helrunar

d. Nevermore

141.

Which statement about H.I.M. frontman Ville Valo is false?

a. Ville Valo loves riding motorcycles

b. Ville Valo is a talented skateboarder

c. Ville Valo is a talented painter

d. Ville Valo loves literature

142.

a. In Flames' The Jester Race is often mentioned with subsequent albums of the same genre. Which album doesn't fit?

b. At The Gates - Slaughter Of The Soul

c. Dark Tranquility – The Gallery

d. Suffocation – Breeding The Spawn

e. Soilwork – Natural Born Chaos

143.

Sort these four Iron Maiden albums by release. Oldest album first. The most recent album last!

a. Powerslave

b. Fear Of The Dark

c. Iron Maiden

d. The Book Of Souls

144.

Which of the following songs is not by Judas Priest?

a. Painkiller

b. Neon Knights

c. Breaking The Law

d. Screaming For Vengeance

145.

Who was the singer on the second Katatonia album Brave Murder Day?

a. Nick Holmes

b. Jonas Renkse

c. Peter Tägtgren

d. Mikael Akerfeldt

146.

What do people often say after Korn?

a. With eight band members, that's clearly too many musicians

b. Why do all band members have a korn tattoo

c. They are the founders of Nu Metal

d. The waiting time of 8 years between the debut album and the second work was too long

147.

Which Kreator album is also known as After The Attack?

a. Pleasure To Kill

b. Endless pain

c. Terrible Certainly

d. Extreme aggression

148.

The third album from Lake Of Tears – A Crimson Cosmos impresses with its surprising sound. Which two subgenres have the Swedes mixed here?

a. Black and death metal

b. Gothic metal and psychedelic rock

c. Doom and Funeral Doom Metal

d. Schlager and Country

149.

Sort these four Linkin Park albums by release. Oldest album first. The most recent album last!

a. Hybrid Theory

b. Meteora

c. A Thousand Suns

d. The Hunting Party

150.

_____ is still the most successful Machine Head album of all time. Complete this sentence!

a. Burn My Eyes

b. Through The Ashes Of Empires

c. The Blackening

d. The More Things Change...

151.

Which of these subgenres is the oldest?

a. New Wave Of British Heavy Metal

b. Thrash metal

c. Death metal

d. Nu metal

152.

Which band position in the entire Manowar band history has not even been filled with a new musician?

a. Drums

b. guitar

c. bass

d. Vocals

153.

Which of these black metal bands comes from the USA?

a. Sarcofargo

b. Mayhem

c. Krieg

d. 1349

154.

Sort these four Megadeath albums by release. Oldest album first. The most recent album last!

a. The Sick, the Dying… and the Dead

b. Peace Sells…But Who's Buying

c. Killing Is My Business… And Business Is Good

d. So Far, So Good… So What

155.

Which Mercyful Fate album still counts as a huge milestone for the band today?

a. Dead again

b. Don't Break The Oath

c. In The Shadows

d. Time

156.

On the two cult Metal Church albums Metal Church (1984) and The Dark (1986) _____ is behind the microphone. Complete this sentence.

a. Mike Howe

b. David Wayne

c. Ronny Munroe

d. Marc Lopes

157.

When did Metallica bassist Cliff Burton die?

a. 1984

b. 1985

c. 1986

d. 1987

158.

Which statement about the Portuguese band Moonspell is true?

a. In Portugal, a street was named after the singer

b. The Portuguese Post has released a Moonspell stamp

c. None of their albums have been released in Portugal

d. In Portugal, a public square was named after the band

159.

What is special about the Morbid Angels records?

a. They are without lyrics

b. The singer painted all the covers himself

c. They are arranged consecutively alphabetically

d. It's not available on vinyl

160.

a. What is the name of the last official Motörhead album?

b. Bad magic

c. Aftershock

d. inferno

e. Motörizer

161.

On which album did My Dying Bride singer Aaron Strainthorpe for the first time almost completely abandon his deep growls?

a. As The Flower Withers

b. The Angel And The Dark River

c. Turn Loose The Swans

d. God Is Alone (EP)

162.

The American death metal band Macabre sing exclusively about...?

a. politics

b. Actor

c. Serial killers

d. about other bands

163.

The Swedish death black metal band Necrophobic named themselves after a song by...?

a. Slayer

b. Metallica

c. Anthrax

d. Megadeth

164.

The death metal cult album From Beyond is by...?

a. Massacre

b. Cancer

c. Pungent Stench

d. Hobbs Angel Of Death

165.

The first singer of the band Nightwish was called?

a. Floor Jansen

b. Anette Olzon

c. Tarja Turunen

d. Elize Ryd

166.

The cover artwork for the Obituary record Cause Of Death was actually intended for the thrash metal band _____. Complete this sentence.

a. Kreator

b. Cannibal Corpse

c. Slayer

d. Sepultura

167.

When did Opeth's legendary Blackwater Park appear?

a. 1985

b. 1999

c. 2001

d. 2015

168.

Which of the following Thrash Metal records is not from Overkill?

a. The New Order

b. Under The Influence

c. The Years Of Decay

d. The Electric Age

169.

Who wasn't a founding member of Black Sabbath?

a. Toni Iommi

b. Ozzy Osbourne

c. Vinnie Appice

d. Bill Ward

170.

Which Pantera album really exists?

a. Cowboys From Steel

b. Vulgar Display Of Trendkill

c. Vulgar Display Of Power

d. Far Beyond Hell

171.

The most famous Paradise Lost song to date is probably _____. Complete this sentence.

a. Gothic

b. opium

c. All Alone

d. For My Fallen Angel

172.

Why is Possessed frontman Jeff Becerra in a wheelchair?

a. He had a car accident

b. He hasn't been able to walk since birth

c. He was attacked on the street and shot

d. It fell from the window of a fourth floor apartment

173.

Rammstein is one of the top German rock and metal exports of the last twenty years, but is there a band that is even more successful?

a. Kreator

b. Scorpions

c. Accept

d. Helloween

174.

What is the name of the debut album by the Swedish power metal band Sabaton?

a. Carolus Rex

b. The Great War

c. Attero Dominatus

d. Primo Victoria

175.

On which Saint Vitus album can you find the songs Dying Inside, Clear Windowpane and Thirsty And Miserable?

a. Saint Vitus

b. Born Too Late

c. Hallows Victim

d. Lillie: F-65

176.

Which statement about Sarcofago mastermind Wagner Antichrist Lamounier is correct?

a. He does not live in Brazil all year round

b. He's actually a professor of economics

c. He has a helicopter license

d. He is still a member of Sepultura

177.

What is the name of Saturnus' debut album?

a. Paradise Belongs To You

b. Veronika Decides To Die

c. Martyrs

d. The Storm Within

178.

Which mixture of statements about Saxon is correct?

a. You come from France, your debut album was called Saxon, the singer is Peter Byford

b. Originally called Son Of A Bitch, Wheels Of Steel is an album by them, they come from Barnsley

c. They come from Great Britain, one of their albums is called Denim And Leather, they play death metal

d. You come from Great Britain, one of your albums is called Mutter, the singer is Lemmy Kilmister

179.

Which album gave Sepultura their big breakthrough?

a. Sepultura

b. Kairos

c. Beneath The Remains

d. Arise

180.

Six Feet Under mastermind Chris Barnes used to be a singer with…?

a. Deicide

b. Obituary

c. Cannibal Corpse

d. Morbid Angel

181.

What was the name of the Skid Row singer on the self-titled debut album?

a. Sebastian Bach

b. Sebastian Mozart

c. Sebastian Beethoven

d. Sebastian Holst

182.

Who was never a band member of Slayer?

a. Kirk Hammett

b. Gary Holt

c. Paul Bostaph

d. Jeff Hanneman

183.

What special characteristics do the band members of Slipknot have?

a. They all have short hair

b. They all have green t-shirts

c. They all have glasses

d. They all have masks

184.

Which German trash metal cult record is from Sodom?

a. Extreme aggression

b. Agent Orange

c. The Morning After

d. Infernal overkill

185.

Which band isn't from Iceland?

a. Solstafir

b. The Vintage Caravan

c. Tyr

d. Kaleo

186.

Which band did cult figure Max Cavalera never participate in?

a. Sepultura

b. Killers Be Killed

c. Nail bomb

d. Suicidal Angels

187.

The brutal death metallers Suffocation's debut album is called?

a. Souls To Deny

b. Effigy Of The Forgotten

c. The Ten Commandments

d. Stillborn

188.

Where are the roots of System Of A Down?

a. Kazakhstan

b. Armenia

c. Azerbaijan

d. Bulgaria

189.

What are most Tankard songs about?

a. Of politics

b. Of alcohol

c. Of serial killers

d. Of social injustices

190.

Sort these four Testament albums by release. Oldest album first. The most recent album last.

a. The Formation Of Damnation

b. The Legacy

c. Brotherhood Of The Snake

d. Practice What You Preach

191.

The doom metal album Psalm 9 is by…?

a. Pentagram

b. Saint Vitus

c. Trouble

d. Candlemass

192.

Which statement in the Type O Negative universe is false?

a. Peter Steele was once in Playgirl magazine

b. All members of the band had to tattoo the band logo

c. Before Type O Negative, Peter Steele was in a thrash metal band called Carnivore

d. Peter Steele was a relatively small man at 1.55 meters

193.

When you hear the names and titles Cronos, Black Metal and Countless Bathory most metalheads immediately think of...?

a. Venom

b. Celtic Frost

c. Metallica

d. Rammstein

194.

Dokken is an American _____.
Complete this sentence.

a. Thrash and speed metal band

b. Heavy and glam metal band

c. Black and death metal band

d. Country and folk metal band

195.

What else does Rob Zombie do besides music...?

a. He sells records in a record store

b. He is a passionate writer

c. He is a talented landscape painter

d. He makes Hollywood films

196.

Which of these records is no longer considered classic doom metal, but rather death doom?

a. Born Too Late

b. Psalm 9

c. Be forewarned

d. The Dreadful Hours

197.

Ahab is a German...?

a. Black metal band

b. Funeral Doom Metal Band

c. Thrash metal band

d. Heavy metal band

198.

Before Tobias Sammett celebrated great success with Avantasia, he founded the band...?

a. Helloween

b. Grave Digger

c. Edguy

d. Accept

199.

After Kai Hansen left Helloween he founded _____. Complete this sentence.

a. Edguy

b. Sabaton

c. Gammaray

d. Blind Guardian

200.

Which Grave Digger album is not part of a Trilogy?

a. Heavy Metal Breakdown

b. Tunes Of War

c. Knight Of The Cross

d. Excalibur

201.

Antigone, Veto and Wanderer are albums by...?

a. Caliban

b. As I Lay Dying

c. Heaven Shall Burn

d. Parkway Drive

202.

The thrash metal band Holy Moses surprised people back in 1986 with...?

a. satanic texts

b. their mix of black and thrash metal

c. with a female thrash metal singer

d. with a two man band

203.

Which band had great success from the 2000s onwards with Blood Of The Saints, Preachers Of The Night and Blessed & Possessed?

a. Amon Amarth

b. Sabaton

c. Ghost

d. Powerwolf

204.

Rock n Rolf is the nickname of the singer of which band?

a. Accept

b. Running wild

c. Scorpions

d. Rammstein

205.

Doro is a cult figure, especially in German metal. At the end of the 1980s she made her breakthrough with the band _____? Complete this sentence.

a. Warlock

b. Girl school

c. Suzi Quatro Band

d. Holy Moses

SOLUTIONS

1) c
2) b
3) d
4) a
5) b, a, d, c
6) d
7) d
8) a
9) c
10) a
11) b, c, d, a
12) b
13) c
14) a
15) d
16) d
17) b
18) c
19) d
20) a

21) b
22) d
23) a
24) c
25) b
26) d
27) b
28) a
29) c
30) a
31) d
32) d
33) b
34) c
35) a
36) a
37) d, b, a, c
38) c
39) b
40) b
41) a
42) d
43) b

44) c
45) a
46) d
47) b
48) c
49) d
50) a
51) a
52) a
53) c
54) d
55) b
56) c
57) b, d, c, a
58) a
59) a
60) c
61) d
62) c
63) b
64) a
65) c
66) b

67) a
68) c
69) d
70) d
71) c
72) d
73) b
74) d, c, a, b
75) a
76) b
77) b
78) a
79) b
80) c
81) a
82) d
83) c
84) b
85) a, c, b, d
86) c
87) c
88) a
89) d

90) b
91) c
92) c
93) c
94) a
95) b
96) d
97) c
98) d
99) b
100) a
101) c
102) b
103) d
104) a
105) c
106) b
107) c
108) d
109) b
110) a
111) c
112) a

113) a
114) d
115) d
116) b
117) c
118) a, b, d, c
119) d
120) c
121) b
122) c
123) a
124) c
125) d
126) b
127) d
128) a
129) d
130) b
131) c
132) a
133) b
134) b
135) d

136) c
137) a
138) b
139) c
140) d
141) b
142) c
143) c, a, b, d
144) b
145) d
146) c
147) a
148) b
149) a, b, c, d
150) a
151) a
152) d
153) c
154) c, b, d, a
155) b
156) b
157) c
158) b

159) d
160) a
161) b
162) c
163) a
164) a
165) c
166) d
167) c
168) a
169) c
170) c
171) a
172) c
173) b
174) d
175) b
176) b
177) a
178) b
179) d
180) c
181) a

182) a
183) d
184) b
185) c
186) d
187) b
188) b
189) b
190) b, d, a, c
191) c
192) d
193) a
194) b
195) d
196) d
197) b
198) c
199) c
200) a
201) c
202) c
203) d
204) b

205) a

Printed in Great Britain
by Amazon